Xenofeminism

Theory Redux

Alfie Bown, *The Playstation Dreamworld*

Laurent de Sutter, *Narcocapitalism*

Roberto Esposito, *Persons and Things*

Graham Harman, *Immaterialism: Objects and Social Theory*

Helen Hester, *Xenofeminism*

Srećko Horvat, *The Radicality of Love*

Dominic Pettman, *Infinite Distraction: Paying Attention to Social Media*

Nick Srnicek, *Platform Capitalism*